Tim Fraser

# Candy

# Salamander Street

PLAYS

First published in 2023 by Salamander Street Ltd., a Wordville imprint. (info@salamanderstreetcom).

*Candy* © Tim Fraser, 2023

Cover photography by Athena Bounti and Faidon Loumakis.

ISBN: 9781914228926

10 9 8 7 6 5 4 3 2 1

Further copies of this publication can be purchased from www.salamanderstreet.com

Wordville

*Candy* was first performed at the King's Head Theatre on 19th January 2020. Will was played by Michael Waller. The play is based on a short play first performed on 10th March 2017 at London's Soho Theatre. In that production, Will was played by Wilf Scolding.

# WRITER'S THANKS:

I would like to thank my collaborators Michael Waller and Nico Rao Pimparé, who encouraged me to expand Will's story from a six-page monologue to a one-act play, and who have directed and produced and performed my ramblings in various venues with so much commitment since then. Without you, none of this would have happened. Michael the multi-tasker, I am convinced you are superhuman.

Thank you to every theatre that has staged the play, and to the rest of Team Candy – including Mike Cottrell, Stephen Waller, Rosie Evans-Hill, Athena Bounti and Faidon Loumakis – for helping bring the story from page to stage.

Thank you to everyone who, with their feedback and encouragement, helped the different versions of *Candy* develop over the years; especially to Brian Ward, Kirsty Patrick Ward, Wilf Scolding, Sam Steiner, Haleema Mirza, Lucy Sneddon, Angie Moneke, Niall Webster, Guen Murroni and Stewart Pringle.

Thank you to The Magnetic Fields for writing the song 'Andrew in Drag'.

Finally, thank you to my family, especially my Mum and Dad, for their tireless support and encouragement. I love you.

# CAST AND CREW

### Tim Fraser | Writer

*Candy* is Tim Fraser's debut play. With Sarah Soh, he is the co-writer of *Juniper Mae*, a series of illustrated children's books published by Flying Eye Books. Tim was part of BBC Writersroom's London Voices in 2022 and has an MA in Screenwriting from the NFTS.

### Nico Rao Pimparé | Director

Nico is a British-Indian-French director for stage and screen. As a theatre director, his credits include *Diary of a Somebody* (Seven Dials Playhouse), *Rainer* (Arcola Theatre), *Candy* (Underbelly, King's Head Theatre, Blue Elephant Theatre/ZOOTV, Park Theatre), *Reboot: Shorts 2, The Interpretation of Dreams* (Bunker Theatre), *Jules César* (Voice4Thought International Festival, Dakar), *Dead Souls* (Theatre N16) and *Nozdryov* (Young Vic, Freshworks). Student productions include *Three Sisters* (LAMDA) and *The Great Stage* (East 15). His film work includes *The Start of Nothing* (short) and *They Just Use The Sky* (short). Nico is also an actor, with credits in Hollywood, UK and European TV and film productions, and theatres across the UK.

### Michael Waller | Producer & Actor *(Will)*

Michael's theatre credits include *Candy* (UK Tour, Underbelly/Edinburgh Fringe, ZOOTV/Edinburgh Fringe, King's Head Theatre), *Reboot: Shorts 1 and 2* (Bunker Theatre), *Love and Money, Macbeth: Reboot*, and *Stace in Space* (Vaults Festival). Michael is the co-founder and producer of Reboot Theatre Company and also works as a respiratory doctor specialising in cystic fibrosis.

### Alys Whitehead | Set and Costume Design Consultant

Alys Whitehead is a Scenographer based in London and the South East. She likes working with new and abstract writing and is passionate about making work thoughtfully, with a particular aim to be as sustainable and waste-free as possible. She is an Associate Designer of Dissident Theatre and NDT Broadgate.

As designer, theatre includes: *Sorry We Didn't Die At Sea* (Park); *Snowflakes* (Park); *The Retreat* (Finborough); *Lysistrata* (Lyric Hammersmith); *SAD* (Omnibus); *Maddie* (Arcola). As associate designer, theatre includes: *Wordplay* (Royal Court); *Zoe's Peculiar Journey Through Time* (Theatre Rites/ Southbank Centre & International Tour); *Sea Creatures* (Hampstead). As assistant designer, theatre includes: *Dixon and Daughters* (National).

## Jonathan Chan  |  Lighting Designer

Jonathan trained at Guildhall School of Music and Drama. His credits include: *Love Bomb* (NYT), *Duck* (Arcola), *Grindr: The Opera* (Union), *Snowflakes* (Park & Old Red Lion), *All Roads* (London Tour), *Get Happy* (Pleasance), *Emmeline* (UK Tour), *In the Net* (Jermyn Street), *Grandad Me and Teddy Too* (Polka), *The Solid Life of Sugar Water* (Orange Tree), *Heroin to Hero* (Edinburgh Fringe), *Move Fast* and *Break Things* (Camden People's & Edinburgh Fringe), *Pussycat In Memory of Darkness*, *The Straw Chair* (Finborough), *Maybe Probably, Belvedere* (Old Red Lion), *Different Owners at Sunrise* (The Roundhouse), *Barstools to Broadway, Amphibian* (King's Head), *Sticks & Stones, Time, Random* (Tristan Bates), *Urinetown: the Musical, Opera Makers* (Guildhall School), *Fidelio* (Glyndebourne - Assistant Lighting Designer) and *The Passenger* R&D (Guildhall - Associate Lighting Designer).

## Anna Short  |  Sound Designer

Anna trained at LAMDA.

Theatre credits as Sound Designer include *Lady Dealer* (Roundabout, Summerhall); *Bad Ladz* (Studio at New Wimbledon Theatre); *Spy for Spy* (Riverside Studios); *Primary Shakespeare: As You Like It* (Orange Tree Theatre); *Crackers* (Polka Theatre); *Ravenscourt* (Hampstead Theatre); *Press / 4* (Park Theatre); *Seven Celebrations* (Orange Tree Theatre); *Don't Smoke in Bed* (VAULT); *Nothing on Earth* (UK Tour); *In This Smoking Chaos* (Queen's Theatre Hornchurch); *Camp Albion* (Watermill Theatre/UK Tour); *I Know I Know I Know* (Southwark Playhouse); *The Straw Chair* (Finborough Theatre).

As Co-Sound Designer: *Get Happy* (Pleasance Theatre).

As Associate Sound Designer: *My Son's a Queer* (But What Can You Do?) (Turbine Theatre); *Folk* (Hampstead Theatre); *Lesbian Space Crime* (Soho Theatre); *Two Billion Beats* (Orange Tree Theatre).

## Fae Hochgemuth | Stage Manager

Originally from Amsterdam, Fae is a freelance Stage Manager who studied at the MBO Theaterschool Rotterdam and worked on multiple productions at the International Theatre Amsterdam, including *A Little Life* (Ivo van Hove), *Falling Man* (Julien Gosselin), and *Death in Venice* (Ramsey Nasr) as well as doing a National tour of *Showponies II: de Alex Klaasen Revue* (Gijs de Lange). After graduating from the Stage Management course at the Royal Central School of Speech and Drama she has worked as a Production Manager at Ugly Duck, an Assistant Stage Manager on *Farm Hall* (Stephen Unwin), Stage Manager on *Paper Cut* and is delighted to work on *Candy*.

# PARK THEATRE

## ABOUT PARK THEATRE

Park Theatre was founded by Artistic Director, Jez Bond and Creative Director Emeritus, Melli Marie. The building opened in May 2013 and, with 12 West End transfers, two National Theatre transfers and 14 national tours in ten years, quickly garnered a reputation as a key player in the London theatrical scene. Park Theatre has received six Olivier nominations, won numerous Off West End Offie Awards, and won The Stage's Fringe Theatre of the Year and Accessible Theatre Award.

---

Park Theatre is an inviting and accessible venue, delivering work of exceptional calibre in the heart of Finsbury Park. We work with writers, directors and designers of the highest quality to present compelling, exciting and beautifully told stories across our two intimate spaces.

Our programme encompasses a broad range of work from classics to revivals with a healthy dose of new writing, producing in-house as well as working in partnership with emerging and established producers. We strive to play our part within the UK's theatre ecology by offering mentoring, support and opportunities to artists and producers within a professional theatre-making environment.

Our Creative Learning strategy seeks to widen the number and range of people who participate in theatre, and provides opportunities for those with little or no prior contact with the arts.

In everything we do we aim to be warm and inclusive; a safe, welcoming and wonderful space in which to work, create and visit.

★★★★★ "A five-star neighbourhood theatre." The Independent

As a registered charity [number 1137223] with no public subsidy, we rely on the kind support of our donors and volunteers. To find out how you can get involved visit parktheatre.co.uk

## FOR PARK THEATRE

**Artistic Director** Jez Bond
**Interim Executive Director** Vanessa Lefrancois

---

Creative Learning

**Community Engagement Manager** Carys Rose Thomas
**Creative Learning Leaders** Amy Allen, Joshua Picton, Kieran Rose, Vanessa Sampson

---

Development

**Development Director** Tania Dunn
**Development & Producing Assistant** Ellen Harris

---

Finance

**Finance Director** Elaine Lavelle
**Finance & Administration Officer** Nicola Brown

---

General Management

**General Manager** Tom Bailey
**Producer Programmer** Amelia Cherry
**Access Coordinator** David Deacon
**Administrator** Mariah Sayer
**Duty Venue Managers** Leiran Gibson, Gareth Hackney, Zara Naeem, Laura Riseborough, Natasha Green, David Hunter, Shaun Joynson, Leena Makoff, Wayne Morris, Daisy Bates, Nick Raistrick

---

Park Café & Bar

**Supervisors** Eli Powell, Daisy Bates
**Bar Team** George Gehm, John Burman, Francesca Fratichenti, Alex Kristoffy, Isabella Meyersohn, Maddie Stoneman, Bonni Shapland-Hill

---

Sales & Marketing

**Sales & Marketing Director (Maternity Leave)** Dawn James
**Sales & Marketing Director (Maternity Cover)** Sammie Squire
**Sales & Ticketing Manager** Matthew Barker
**Senior Marketing Officer** Anna Charlesworth

Tim Fraser

# Candy

# CHARACTERS

*Candy* is a monologue performed by one man, who interacts with the audience.

The performer should feel free to feed off the audience's reactions, even if it means changing parts of the script. A little bit of ad-libbing is encouraged.

A new paragraph indicates a beat.

## WILL:

Twenty-something, South Yorkshire accent, motor-mouthed.

Will is good-looking, relaxed and charismatic, with a dry wit that helps put the audience at ease. Underneath this exterior, he is unsatisfied and unhappy. But it's well-hidden; he has had years of practice masking his emotions, so it's a very convincing mask (despite the cracks, which widen as his story plays out).

# 1.

*Lights up on WILL, who stands in the middle of the stage.*

*The stage is empty apart from a live microphone on a stand to one side of him, and perhaps some chairs. WILL addresses the audience.*

**WILL:** I never really got the phrase: "Love at first sight."

I mean, it don't mean nowt, it's just words, in't it. Just summat to say at your wedding to make you sound dead romantic.

I always thought, 'why can't people see past the bullshit?'

Groom's like, 'oh, it were love at first sight I tell ya!' Bride interrupts him like, 'no it weren't you knobhead – you tried to get with me mate and, when she rejected you, you jumped on my face because you're a randy fucker.'

Maybe not that suitable for the kids at the ceremony. More honest, though.

Anyway, I'm getting ahead of myself. We all having a nice evening, ladies and gents?

*He waits half a beat for a response.*

Yeah? Good, good. So, love at first shite, right. Romeo and Juliet. Remember reading it at school, thinking, 'what's he doing marrying someone he's only known for, like, a day?' He hasn't even asked her what she's into! What if he's, like, into art and books and things, and Juliet just likes getting bladdered, doing lines and chatting shit?

OK, not the most relevant examples to the text... Err... what if Romeo's all about Renaissance composers like Orlando de Lassus, but Juliet's, like, into lute music or summat? They could never go to the same gigs.

*WILL catches the eye of a woman in the audience.*

Oh, you liked that didn't ya? Orlando de Lassus. Not just a pretty face, me. I know stuff. Know how to Google stuff.

*He turns his attention back to the whole audience.*

Anyway, so, I didn't believe it...

I *really* didn't fucking believe it. Until I saw her...

It were at me mate's gig. I weren't even gonna go.

*He launches into an impression of his mate.*

'Aw, please mate, come' – that's me mate Billy.

He's just moved back here from London. He was gigging a lot down there with his new band. Last time I saw him on stage was when we was eighteen. I just think it's a bit sad. He hasn't really moved on.

*(as BILLY again)* 'Aw, mate, please.'

*(talking to an imaginary BILLY)* Uhh, I dunno, mate.

*(as BILLY)* 'Why? What else are you gonna do?'

Unfortunately, all that comes to me head is the truth, and I don't think he'd be best pleased if I say: 'Playing Call of Duty Vanguard all night'...

*(baffled, to an audience member who looks like they probably play video games)* You played it? It's set in World War II, right, but you can play as Snoop Dogg. Like, you're literally Snoop Dogg, in a pimp coat, shooting Nazis... It's fucking mental.

Anyway, I know none of that'll fly so say 'alright then' and I go.

Mainly out of loyalty though. First friend I made at school, Billy was. I were the new lad. Moved down from Chorfield to me Mum's hometown after me Dad mustered up the courage to tell her:

*(as his DAD, a very matter-of-fact man)* 'Thank you ever so much for the fifteen years of marriage but – after careful consideration – I regret to inform you that I don't fuckin' love you anymore. Also, I'm taking the pepper grinder.'

Met Billy on the first day of term. It's weird starting in Year Eight with a bunch of strangers. I was so pissed off that I were even _there_. Like, I'd just started getting used to all them other kids and now everyone was different. But _they_ all knew each other. It didn't feel fair.

They even got me up and did that whole embarrassing–

_(impression of an overly cheery female teacher, perhaps with a Scottish accent)_ 'This is Will, he's new. Please say hi to him and make him feel welcome – even though by singling him out, I'm only increasing his chances of being beaten the shit out of later, because I'm making him stand here while everyone else is sat down staring at him, and there is literally no way to be in that position and not look like a total prick.'

Not bitter.

I'm not sure if she sat me next to him because we were both Williams, or if it's cos he were the only kid who had an empty seat next to him.

He were an awkward lad. Didn't even look up at me, just carried on drawing in his little notebook. He were a bit tubby, greasy hair, ill-fitting uniform. He didn't try to make his tie as short and fat as possible like the other lads.

I took one look at his normal-lengthed tie and thought 'what a fucking freak.'

Then I looked down and saw what he were drawing. It were really good – like, he had talent and that – but it were literally a giraffe, but instead of having a head it had a toothbrush head?

He saw me looking and for the first time seemed to notice I were there.

I said, _(pointing at the imagined drawing)_ 'What's that you got there?'

He looked at me like I were dense: 'Giraffe... with a toothbrush head.'

'I can see it's a giraffe with a toothbrush head, I mean why are you drawing a giraffe with a toothbrush head?'

(*he shrugs as BILLY*) 'Started drawing giraffe and thought I'd make its head a toothbrush.'

And that were Billy.

He didn't fit in with the other lads. But when he were sixteen he began to wash his hair regularly, lost his puppy fat, and started playing in a band. Jangly guitar music was cool again and suddenly we all wanted to be mates with an indie rock star. We'd go see him play every Friday night...

Fast-forward however many years later and it's a different story. I mean, here I am at this gig and I don't know anyone. None of our mates from school are here. Plus I'm a bit late – Billy's already getting ready in the green room – can't introduce me to anyone.

I stand around for ages with a pint in me hand, looking like a pillock. I'm all riled up – I wouldn't have come if I'd known it were a fiver to get in. Plus admin fee! This really fit bird gives me a funny look, like I'm a weirdo, so I go up to the front. Pretend I'm eagerly awaiting the band's grand entrance. Just standing there, thinking of all the Nazis I could be wasting right now with Snoop Dogg's finishing move that they've actually named Finishizzle Movizzle, trying to look cool, like:

*He does an impression of himself, staring gormlessly at an imagined stage, an imagined drink in his hand, checking his imaginary watch.*

*He milks this.*

Anyway, eventually the lights go down. I'm like, 'finally!' Everyone cheers and claps. The band comes up on stage – three of Billy's mates. But then... <u>she</u> arrives.

*His eyes widen, his voice fills with wonder.*

She wears this... long, flowing red dress. Her arms are poised high up in the air as she catwalks to the front of the stage.

Icy blue eyes, blonde curly hair to her shoulders – proper elegant – like she's floating...

She's the most beautiful woman I've ever seen in my life. But it's more than that. She's got... *grace*. She commands the room, but at the same time she's inviting you in.

*He pauses, sighs.*

Now, I'm not mad; I know it's Billy in a fucking dress. I know that. The rational side of me knows that, but my *heart*! It stops. My lip trembles, there's goosebumps all over me body. She smiles, and I don't see Billy – but I feel as if I *know* her. As sexy and unique as she is, there's summat about her that's *familiar*. Like a cup of tea, or the smell of home.

You know what, that's it. I look at her, and it's like coming home. It's like I've arrived.

And I think that all my years on Earth were leading up to this moment, where she extends her hand and – finger-by-finger – grasps the microphone like it's hers, and in the smokiest voice you've ever heard, says: (*into the microphone*) 'Hello. I'm Candy.'

*He lets CANDY's words hang for a long beat.*

*Shrugs at the audience.*

Love at first sight.

*He becomes very aware of everyone in front of him.*

Full disclosure – this is a *woman* in front of me, right? Not some bloke in cheap lipstick and fake eyelashes – no... A proper, proper woman. I don't know what Billy's done but it's a complete transformation, and I can't deny how I feel.

I spend the whole gig watching her, wrestling with myself, like:

*He becomes two versions of himself who debate with each other.*

(*as WILL 1*) 'Will, that's Billy. That's fucking Billy.'

(*as WILL 2*) 'What? No! Look at her, Will! This ain't Billy. She ain't Billy.'

And as I'm thinking this the band's playing, and Candy starts singing this ballad. This heartfelt ballad – proper slow and emotional, and summat changes.

My thoughts stop and it's just me, alone with her, as she sings. I'm not being funny but her voice, it has this sadness – like she's letting me into her head and telling me:

(*as CANDY, into the mic*) 'Hold me. I need ya'.

*He gulps, emotional. The memory haunts him.*

And I'm listening and I'm crying into my pint and I don't know why but right now I don't care – I just know that this is the best song I've ever heard in my fucking life, and if I can't cry now then when the fuck can I.

So I cry. I cry and I clap till my hands _burn_. I scream along with the rest of them.

Candy's smiling, laughing – she knows she fucking aced it. Then she... she catches my eye and she winks at me.

Nothing else matters. Candy's eyes _met mine._

Candy's eyes. Billy's eyes. But Billy's never looked at me like that. I don't know if it were the eye make-up or the fact that she singled me out and had the gall to fucking wink at me – but in that moment it weren't Billy. It just weren't.

*He shuffles his trousers in his pockets.*

As she keeps singing I can't stop thinking about that moment. All the blood rushing to my...

*He stops shuffling, suddenly aware of what he's doing.*

...head.

And then... it's over. Candy leaves the stage and I'm alone again.

Five minutes later, Billy comes back. Simple as that. Candy is dead, and Billy has been reborn in her ashes.

(*as BILLY*) 'Hey man! Good to see ya! Glad you could make it! Enjoy the show?'

*WILL gives a disparaging look to the audience.*

(*as himself*) Yeah, it were good, Billy. Proper good, mate, well done.

(*as BILLY*) 'Oh fantastic, cheers man.'

(*as himself, under his breath*) Murderer.

(*as BILLY*) 'What?'

(*as himself*) Nothing.

*WILL shrugs at the audience.*

I leave pretty soon after that. Don't go home straight away – wander the streets for a bit – thinking. Don't know what to do with myself.

I mean, should I tell him?

What would he think of me? What do I think of me? I mean – that were Billy! Fuckin' Billy Glover.

In the end I kinda just... carry on. Work, weekends, wanking. You know – life. Try to get the whole thing out of me head.

But that's the thing about your head. It makes them decisions for you, dunnit.

Deleted all my social media accounts years ago, but I find myself undeleting them – because apparently that's a thing you can do – just so I can see pictures of her. Endlessly swiping through the same few pictures...

I sit at my desk, daydreaming at work, imagining where Candy is and what she's doing. Till I remember Candy's blonde hair's probably in a drawer somewhere, her dress hanging up to dry in Billy's room, and I shiver, like:

*WILL shudders audibly.*

*(he does an impression of a keen middle-aged woman)* Debra says 'oh are you cold, Will? I'll close the window.'

That's my boss. She likes me. Maybe a bit too much.

Our office for some reason has these really high ceilings, right, so like the windows are really – you have to stand on a chair to open them, basically. So Debra clambers onto this office chair, the wheels making it swivel, and she starts shaking her hips to try and balance on the chair like–

*He does an impression of this, shaking his hips, trying to balance and close the window at the same time, making little 'ooh' sounds as DEBRA as he does.*

I'm like 'it's alright Debra – I en't cold, I were just remembering that this lass I'm infatuated with is essentially an elaborate Instagram filter on a bloke' – except I only say that first bit.

But then I see how much her hips are gyrating and I think hang on, is she doing this for me? And then for the briefest of moments I imagine our lips touching and I shudder way harder than before.

*He becomes DEBRA again, gyrating rhythmically.*

*(looking back at WILL)* 'Not cold?! Look at you shivering, lad.'

*DEBRA closes the window, letting out a little 'eh' noise.*

*He laughs at his impression, becoming WILL again.*

I been working there for the best part of five years now. It's a little car insurance company in town. Boring as fuck most of the time. People there come and go, and the ones who don't are like the living equivalents of a shrug.

But when I get a sale through I still get a little jump in me heart like 'let's have it!' And it's alright chatting to people and that. I suppose it's what I'm best at. Well, I know it is – Debra lets me just get on with it these days. Occasionally when she's walking round the office she looks up at my sales tally on the white board and does this.

*WILL gives the double thumbs up and makes a strained face of approval to someone in the audience.*

But it's different today. In hindsight I think Debra only closes the window cos she saw I'm off me game and is trying to figure out why? I don't blame her, I mean I've done shifts on the mother of all hangovers, and on all her daughters too, and it never makes no difference.

That one bad shift is enough to set me off. I'm driving home thinking, shit – what's wrong with me? I can't lose this job. Shit.

My life before it – working nights at the pub down the road, drinking with me boss after hours till the sun come up... I can't go back to that.

Reminds me of the summer when we was eighteen. I'd just started working there, but already Geoff were letting me have lock-ins after hours. The last weekend – before me mates all went off to uni – we had a mad one. Billy was the only one going to London. I remember, that night, I said 'Why you going so far away? What's the point?'

He said he always wanted to live in London. I leaned back and said to the lads, 'Aye, he's a southern fairy at heart, our Billy'.

*We can see on his face he regrets saying that.*

But really, I were happy for him. First of his family to go. But it were this art school, so his dad didn't think it were a good idea.

*(as BILLY'S DAD)* 'Oh you're gonna be the next Da Vinci, are ya?'

That's Billy's dad. Tricky man. Terrible moustache.

His art were always really good, and he seemed to know what he were talking about... Toothbrush giraffe notwithstanding.

Made myself laugh imagining that drawing propped up at a London art gallery one day. All these pretentious southerners gathering round it.

*He becomes two versions of himself again, this time looking up at this imaginary artwork.*

(*as SOUTHERNER 1*) 'This is one of the artist's early works.'

(*as SOUTHERNER 2*) 'Ah yes, I think it symbolically symbolises the fragility of the fragile line between society and nature, and the... uh, the...' (*the character has a realisation*) '...it's a fucking giraffe with a toothbrush head. Quentin, I think I've wasted my life.'

*He tries not to but chuckles at his own joke.*

Anyway, judging by me mates' posts, the first few weeks of uni mainly consist of dressing up as daft things, but it stopped eventually. With Billy, it didn't really stop. On occasion he'd use a bit of guyliner on nights out and that, dress a little flamboyantly...

So, there I am on the motorway thinking like – how did he get from *that* to Candy? A lad mucking around to the most beautiful woman I've ever seen. I can't make sense of it.

I get home and me Mum's watching some rom-com with Toadface.

Oh, right – Toadface. That's me Great Aunt. Lives with us. We call her Toadface because...

*He stops mid-sentence, realising it's obvious. Looks at the audience as if to say 'you get it'.*

They've been watching rom-coms together two nights a week the last seven years or so – ever since I started earning enough for me Mum to quit her other job – building up a solid DVD collection of goddawful cack.

Me Mum can take or leave romance after me Dad decided that his limited financial contributions to his own family's well-being were at this point so limited that they might as well stop, so she's mainly in it for the "com" element.

Lord knows what Toadface is in it for. She barely moves her eyes from the telly anyway.

I sit down next to me Mum. Toadface is sat on that ancient sofa chair she lives on, with her permanent frown and thick glasses, furrowing her brow at Rick from The Walking Dead. He's holding up signs to Keira Knightley, telling her he loves her and she's perfect and that.

One of them says: 'At Christmas, you tell the truth'. I've never heard that before – I mean, I have cos god knows how many times I've seen this film – but what I mean is it's not a Christmas tradition like Rick's sign claims. If anything, people lie _more_ at Christmas having to pretend they're interested in their uncle's new accountancy job or smiling and nodding as your Gran says, (*as an old lady*) 'there are just too many of those foreigners about these days.'

But it makes me think about somehow seeing Candy again, somehow smuggling a large cardboard sign into the venue and, as she's singing, holding it up – and it says summat really simple and big but also really beautiful about how much I love her, and–

By this point Keira Knightley has _firmly_ rejected him.

Rick walks away saying 'enough', apparently to himself – not even in front of an audience or nothing, which I feel is a bit weird – and I think, yeah. Enough. Time to give this up, whatever it is. I exhale, and I can feel Candy leaving my body and I'm free.

Toadface just groans. As usual.

*He changes where he is in the space to indicate some time has passed.*

11

I'm about to head out to see the lads. It's been a couple nights and I'm good now. I was getting in me own head, my head filled with rom-coms, letting all these thoughts in that are actually just nonsense. So it's back to normal life. Me being me. Billy being Billy.

*He sighs deeply.*

But that were a weird night, I tell thee.

It's alright at first. But three pints in and I don't see Billy anymore. I just see Candy, dressed as a bloke, pretending to be someone she's not.

I'm standing chatting to me mate Chris, and out the corner of my eye I see Billy handing out these flyers.

I'm like (*to an imaginary BILLY*) what's this?

*WILL perhaps picks up a couple of flyers for the show and hands them to audience members.*

(*as BILLY, to the lads*) 'Definitely come, lads – it were a laugh last time weren't it, Will?'

(*WILL fake smiles and nods*) Mmm!

He reads the flyer in his hands to himself. (*Could be a flyer for the show, could be an invisible flyer.*)

His band are doing a tour of Yorkshire, closing with another gig at that same old working man's club in a couple weeks.

My heart starts racing. I could see her again. I could...

No. It's an itch it's best not to scratch. Look at what happened last time, all because, what – of some dumb... No.

Best to just draw a line under it. It were a weird little bump in my life, but it's over.

*He tries to get himself amped up.*

I'm gonna dive in to work. That whiteboard is gonna run out of space – the amount of sales I'm gonna rack up.

*He has failed to amp himself up. His voice lowers.*

But that night I start dreaming.

I'm not the kinda bloke who remembers his dreams, but when you have the same one night after night it kind of, y'know, sticks in your head.

So, I'm on stage and I'm telling the Candy story. This story. To a room full of strangers.

And then I finish, and everyone claps – (*pointedly, at the audience*) really loudly by the way – the lights go up and I see all your faces, and there –

*He points to a far corner of the room. He goes up to the mic and whispers into it:*

–there's Candy, with tears in her eyes. She stands up... walks down them stairs[1]...

*His finger traces Candy's path.*

...and comes right up to me.

*WILL pulls the mic stand closer to him, like it's CANDY.*

There's this electricity between us. She kisses me. And I'm...

*He closes his eyes and uses the mic stand to act out his dream.*

...I'm touching her body, and I feel down there, and it's smooth, and it's warm, and it's wet... She's all woman, and she's mine....

*He opens his eyes, jerking awake, stepping away from the mic stand. He's alone again; he's gutted.*

And then I wake in a cold sweat.

---

1: or up them stairs/the aisle...depending on the theatre.

She is _coursing through my veins_. And my fears are coming true: I'm fucking it all up at work. I'm taking extended smoking breaks just to avoid talking to anyone, murmuring through phone calls.

(_fake cheesy grin_) 'They can hear your smile!'

That's what Debra always says. She has no idea how to be a manager, she just borrows phrases from the company handbook – like "team player" and "killer instinct."

Her thumbs up has been replaced by this concerned frown whenever she walks past.

I sit at my desk practicing the speech in my head – the speech I'll say to Candy that'll make everything OK. But if I do tell her... (_he trails off._)

Can't I somehow tell Candy and Billy dun't hear it? In my head they're two people, with two brains and two... But that's just a fantasy, in't it.

'I'm sorry Will, I'm gonna have to give you a warning,' Debra says. Whatever.

_He sighs._

I text the lads, asking them if they're gonna come to Billy's gig. I don't think they will. Always been funny about that stuff. Apart from my mate Chris, who finds the idea of Billy dressing up as a lass incredibly amusing. Easy man to please, Chris.

When Billy first came back home from uni for Christmas – we were eighteen, nineteen – the lads had seen them photos of him in the dress-up he did before he went full-Candy... They were merciless to him.

But Billy just shrugged it off, y'know. Same way he always did. But this time you could tell he really didn't give a shit about what they thought anymore.

I remember, after a couple, I said to him, (_drunk, accusatory – maybe he grabs a pint out of an audience member's hand for this bit for added authenticity_) 'Think London's changing you, mate.'

His face barely even moved as he told me he'd not changed at all. Started explaining to me – he'd always wanted to do stuff like that, but he knew he could never do it *here*. He were going for it full on at uni cos it were years of him wanting to express this other part of him and he'd stopped himself, right?

I guess it made sense, but still I were like, 'Why do you wanna do it though?'

He said: (*whispering into the mic as BILLY:*) 'It feels... *exciting*. Getting away from myself for a bit. Pretending to be someone else. Whenever me Dad was being a proper dickhead, whenever school was shite, I always... Just to escape. Perform.'

(*away from mic*) Couldn't really say nowt to that. Could've done with some kind of escape myself at that time...

I were still working at that goddawful pub. Only one of me mates not at uni – spending all my free time on social media, scrolling through their far more exciting lives.

*He massages his knuckles, sombre.*

I was punching walls when I were drunk. Which were most of the time. Told myself I didn't want anyone to notice the bruises, but part of me was begging someone to. Anyone.

This one night, I stayed for afters and got so shitfaced that by the time the morning came I thought it'd be a good idea to get the train to Chorfield. I can't remember if it were an impromptu adventure or if I was so pissed I genuinely thought I might still live there... even though we moved when I were twelve.

But as I stood there on the platform, I couldn't stop the thoughts. The fucking noise:

(*as fast and frantic as possible*) 'You've fucked up your life you've fucked up your life you'll never be happy you'll never be happy your best days are over and nothing's in front of you but bills and pain, bills and pain, bills and pain.'

Then I heard the train coming. My heart skipped a beat –
"now or never – fucking do it you coward!" I jumped onto
the tracks...

*He leaves us hanging before defusing the tension with:*

...and watched the train go past me and stop at the platform
opposite.

I were just stood there on the track, swaying a little, feeling
nothing. Can't do anything right.

People were looking at me funny. "Get off the track you
twat," someone shouted, like I were just fooling around. I
mean, I was young and I was smashed – must've been what
it looked like. So I did – I stepped back on the platform and
stumbled back home.

Never told anyone that. I thought about telling Billy that
same night – about how shit it'd all been. It were Christmas
after all and apparently that's when you tell the truth...

*He manages a weak smile, then sighs.*

But we were having fun. He was about to go back to uni –
didn't want him to think of me as the miserable twat stuck
back home while he's off gallivanting in the big smoke.

*Beat.*

*He mimics holding his phone and scrolling through pictures.*

But now here I am, years later. Not nineteen, no. But a
miserable twat once more – on my newly resurrected accounts
every day, pining for Candy.

Photos somehow dun't quite capture her essence – there's
nothing like being there, in her presence. Somehow even
breathing the same air as her were exciting. But it gives me a
little fix.

Then I come off of that high and think about me life –
think about how impossible this is... I mean, I don't even
know what this is. Like, does she even exist? Could she?

*He starts to act and speak frantically.*

Argh, what am I even saying? Am I just in love with Billy?
Do I just wanna be with him and have him dress up the
whole time? I mean, me and me ex did anal, and and and if
Candy wanted to I guess I could just ignore her dick and-
and... (*trails off.*)

I hit Tinder like mad. Distract myself. Get some matches,
give them me best lines, but it just makes me wonder –
'How would Candy respond to this?' I know how Billy would
respond, but I feel like it would be different with her. When
she looked at me, winked at me – when she were singing
them songs... I dunno. She weren't Billy.

But what is she then? A figment of me imagination? It's not
like when I looked up at that stage I magically entered a
world where Billy had a new personality and no dick or balls.

Or... in a way, maybe I did?

*He looks to the audience futilely for an answer. He doesn't get one.*

I know it sounds dumb but these thoughts are whirring
through my head day in day out. I can't get out of bed in the
mornings now. I'm late every day. I snooze my alarm over
and over, hoping to fall asleep again, to see her.

*He moves into a dream. He sees CANDY in front of him.*

It's that same dream again. The electricity. But this time,
when I feel down there there's... something. There's...

But she looks in my eyes and I feel this pull to her. I want to
please her so I touch her and start...

*WILL mimics caressing CANDY's penis.*

It's weird – it's kinda like I'm having a wank with a numb crotch or summat. But then she starts moaning. I mean, when I'm wanking I'm not actually enjoying the action of up and down up and down am I? It's the pleasure the action brings. So, of course I enjoy giving Candy that pleasure. I relish it as she moans and gyrates, faster and louder and higher and I can feel it with her, pulsating with every motion – until–

*He gasps, and moans: he comes. Is he doing an impression of CANDY coming or is he coming himself? Even he's not sure.*

*Silence.*

We look at each other, we're giggling. She stares me in my eyes, strokes my face so so tenderly. I feel this cold wetness on my thigh and I start stirring awake and I'm begging, "Please please, don't wake up, Will. Just one more moment with her, just..."

*He wakes up. Then he looks down at his thigh, surprised.*

Oh... OH.

Now, I _swear_ to you...

*He looks pointedly at an audience member.*

I swear to you... that has not happened to me since I were a teenager.

*He takes a breath.*

I... didn't make it into work that day. Made up some excuse.

The next day, though, Debra calls me into her office. As I go in I look at the state of my sales tally. I'm fucked.

She gives me a right talking to. I nod and look very serious. Promise I'll do better.

But then at the end she asks me: 'Is everything OK?' And she looks in me eyes. I swear I'm about to break.

*He takes the mic stand and shakes it at the sky in defiance as he screams:*

I'M IN LOVE AND IT'S FUCKING AGONY!

I DEFY YOU, STARS!

TOM HANKS! JOHN CUSACK! HUGH FUCKING GRANT! WHY DIDN'T YOU TELL ME LOVE WAS SHITE?! I DEFY YOU ALL!

*WILL takes a beat to calm down a little bit.*

(*under his breath*) Fucking rom-coms.

But I don't say that. I say: 'I don't know.' I think my voice is cracking cos she keeps looking at me, and then she says: 'If there's anything going on, you know you can talk to me. I know I'm your boss but I can be your... *friend* too.'

I think: Christ, Debra, at least buy me a drink first. But then I see how big her eyes are and I know she means it. Years of winking, arse-shaking and light flirting and now she's gunning for a heart-to-heart? I mean it's a little bit in-fucking-congruous, to say the least.

But I have to give her something – that gaze is just too fucking intense, like – and I've ran out of places to avert my eyes.

'Girl trouble' comes out my mouth.

'Ah.' She nods like she knows it well. 'What's her name?'

'Billy,' I say, without thinking.

She says 'Billie Eilish?'

*As DEBRA, WILL laughs: a big fake cackle.*

I don't laugh back. She must be feeling awkward too.

I'm here and I'm in the other corner of the room, looking at my face, and it is *grave*.

*As DEBRA, WILL clears his throat, takes a moment, before saying:*

'I was married, you know. Ten years. He was me high school sweetheart. I didn't like him at first. He was... quiet. But once you got to know him... he were the funniest boy in school. I think, back then, he saw me and saw the life he wanted. I just wanted _him_. It weren't long before I were worshipping every move he made. I ripped up my future plans because none of them mattered: I had _him_.

He didn't want kids, so I didn't. He wanted to stay in Elmsfield, so I did too. As the years got on I could tell that I weren't enough for him anymore. But I wanted him to be OK, so I let him. I let him cry and tell me he was sorry but this was just something he had to do. I sat there. Took it. And he left. And there I was, on me own for the first time, not a clue who I was or what I'd do without him.

Look, Will, I'd like to tell you I had some kind of epiphany and I figured it all out, but that's not what happened. I looked for ways to distract myself, from the pain, I suppose. Focussed on work. And step by step, day by day... And look at me now. Debra Bidwell: Sales Manager. I've got a hot new man on the scene and all. (*proudly*) He's Greek. Well, Albanian, but it's close in't it. And you know what? This time, my life revolves around _me_, not him. But I had to learn to like myself enough to let it.'

*Silence. He looks to the audience.*

Jesus Christ.

I know what she's trying to say but all I hear is that she had _ten years_ with this bloke and she's chastising herself for building her life around him. Meanwhile, one drunken night staring at Candy and I'm having a mental breakdown. Puts it into _sharp_ perspective, ladies and gents.

The thoughts are so loud in my head, but the next thing she says pierces right through the noise.

(*as DEBRA*) 'Do you want to take some time off? Reset?'

She dun't say it like it's a question. 'How about you take the rest of the month off. Come back on the first Monday and we'll have a wee internal review, yeah?' She nods until I nod back.

Shit.

I get home and Toadface is watching Dirty Dancing alone.

It's right at that fucking bit where they're saying they're having the time of their fucking lives.

I launch myself at the eject button and I snap the DVD in half.

*As TOADFACE – crouched down as if sitting on her chair/sat on her chair:*

(*screeching*) 'WILL?? WHAT ON EARTH ARE YOU DOING?'

(*mimicking throwing the snapped DVD*) I take the two pieces and I put that baby in the corner. Suck my dick, Swayze.

(*as TOADFACE*) 'Have you lost your mind? You can't do that! That's my video!'

It's a fucking DVD, you idiot! And what do you know about it? None of it's real. None of this is what love actually is. But you wouldn't know that, would you? You've never loved anything. You're just a sack of emptiness!

She goes silent. I storm off.

*Long beat.*

Few hours later I come down for me Mum's tea and we both act like nothing happened. I can't even look at her, I'm so ashamed.

I tell them – I say what happened at work. Mum's disappointed.

Toadface just nods at me and shoves a forkful of peas in her mouth. I think it were a nod of understanding, but it's hard to tell when you're trying to read a face that looks like an anus and a pug had a really old baby.

Before I know it, it's less than a week till the gig. And I en't gonna go. Nope.

*He shakes his head, trying futilely to convince the audience.*

Not gonna happen.

What? It's not.

Don't look at me like that!

I'm–

*He touches his pocket.*

I'm having a walk in town, just thinking, when my phone buzzes. It's me mum. What's she doing calling me at two in the morning?

(*unconvincingly, to the audience*) I just fancied going for a walk at two in the morning – it's not that I couldn't sleep, or...

*He picks up his imaginary phone.*

Hello?

*WILL does an impression of his MUM, a very thorough woman.*

'Will, it's Mum.'

I know. Your name comes up on my phone, dunnit.

(*as MUM*) 'Will, now's not the time for one of your jokes. Your Great Aunt Geraldine is dead.'

Geraldine?

(*as MUM*) 'Will, don't make me say it.'

(*to audience*) I mean, I only had one Great Aunt, so I really should've guessed, but I'm in me head and it's late, so I say–

Say what?

(*as MUM, sighing through gritted teeth*) 'Toadface.'

Oh, fuck.

(*as MUM*) 'Yeah. Oh fuck.

The first thing I think is that me Mum must've found the body, and that must've been horrible – but it turns out Toadface was at the bingo for the first time in decades. She won and got so excited she had a massive heart attack.

God knows why she were even there.

I'd like to tell you I feel sad, but the truth is I just think, 'Well, that makes sense I suppose.' I mean, she's been old for an eternity.

Bad, innit.

Even worse is the sense of elation I feel when I realise that Toadface's funeral and Candy's gig are on the same day. I have the perfect excuse now. At the pub with Billy I tell him, I'm like:

Look, Billy, as you probably heard, it's me Great Aunt's funeral, so I can't come.

(*as BILLY*) 'Of course mate. But that's in the morning, right? If you fancy a distraction, come down after. We're on at eight thirty.'

(*to the audience*) Bloody hell, this guy's relentless.

I help Mum with the arrangements – get the venue, send the emails, phone everyone. I keep thinking of what I'd said to her. It weren't the last thing I ever said to her – we were civil for days after, like – but that were the impression I left on her, y'know?

What made it worse is knowing no one's gonna come to the funeral, it'll just be me and me Mum and me Nan and me brother John. One or two others – like weird Uncle Derek, who smells like stale air.

Me Mum's gonna go up and say summat. No idea what she's gonna say. I mean, what could you say about Toadface? She watched telly all day every day – I guess you could spin that into a positive?

But then, the morning of it, as I walk downstairs dressed in black, I see Mum and John in the kitchen in black too – and I look to my left and see that old sofa chair she loved so much – still with her fucking arse-print imbedded into it – and I feel... I dunno.

We're the first ones to arrive. But we are early, and as the minutes roll on others come.

And then keep on coming.

Like, it's relatives and that, sure – but people I don't recognise too. I'm not saying it's packed or anything but I ain't seen this many old people in one place since that one time I went to the theatre.

Me Mum's a bit nervous but she says what she says and it's all pleasant enough. But then other people come up to speak – and then at the reception afterwards, speak to me – and they have all these anecdotes!

Anecdotes about "Gerry".

How she'd light up a room, the practical jokes she played, how she would sing. Everyone's going on about how alive she were.

At first I think it's people being nice, y'know, because it's her funeral after all. But then I start noticing this common thing, like: (*as an old man*) 'Oh, I hadn't seen her since Teddy died twenty years ago,' or (*as an old woman*) 'Oh, her and Teddy were so lovely together. She had half a heart without him.'

And there's all these pictures of her there – most of them with me Great Uncle Teddy. She's young. Pretty. Happy.

It's like I finally realise she were this real person. She were Geraldine Pelly.

Calling her Toadface all those years feels a _bit_ wrong now.

It's like Geraldine Pelly died twenty years ago with me Great Uncle Teddy, and Toadface were this husk of her former self that were born into being in that very moment.

And I were the prick who told her she didn't know what love was.

I know I owe her an apology I can never give her. So instead I stay and drink for ages, just listening to these stories, getting steadily more smashed.

I say to me Mum, I say 'I can't believe it.'

She says, 'It makes you think, dun it?'

I'm like, 'yeah. It does. She may've turned into a miserable old bat, but that were only because she knew something that were so much better. This whole time, she were heartbroken, and I didn't know it.'

Me Mum says, 'That's not what I meant.'

But I don't have time to hear it. Because in that instant I know: that could be me. I could be Toadface.

But unlike me Great Aunt, I won't get them _years_ – where I laughed, and I danced, and I sang. I won't even get what Debra got with _her_ husband.

I'll just be miserable, and in the blink of an eye I'll be old and bitter.

(_to his MUM_) Mum. I need to go. Right now.

(_as WILL'S MUM_) 'Right now?'

No, wait. Couple shots for the road.

(_to the audience_) I mean, I'm pissed but I'm still more nervous than pissed, y'know.

Am I really gonna do this? (_He mimics taking a shot_) What will I say? (_Another_) What will I do? (_A final one._)

Am I chasing summat impossible? Summat fictional? Or is it Billy? Is this whole thing just...

But I know I have to try. I'll never forgive myself otherwise. Never.

So I get there. Late. I can hear Candy singing from outside. I rush in, pay the £7.50 to get in – (_annoyed_) it's somehow gone up – and run towards the stage. Right to the front.

_He stares up at her in awe._

And there she is. Same red dress. Same blonde hair... Same eyes.

And I know right then that I've been a _fool_.

Seeing her in motion – of course she's real. Even more real than before.

Her voice soars across the room, light as a feather as I think to myself that if Candy is real – does exist – then she's part of Billy.

She's the, I dunno, the female part, or the part that's hidden away, and I realise – I _know_ – I'm not in love with Billy, I'm in love with that part of him, that little part that, when he gets on stage, transforms into this other entity, this... something-else:

Candy.

And I can feel myself welling up again. I get a tap on me shoulder. It's Chris.

(*as CHRIS, yelling as if over the music*) 'There you are, dickhead! Funny, innit – he's in a dress!'

(*quickly wiping his eyes*) Yeah, mate... Funny.

(*as Chris*) 'Why you in a suit?'

Came from a funeral.

'That's hilarious, mate. You shoulda been here earlier. I made a bet!'

You what?

'I made a bet!'

You made your bed?

(*to the audience*) I were pleased to hear that cos his Mum were still doing it for him.

'No, no, I--'

(*pointing towards the 'stage'*) Maybe we should talk after?

(*to the audience*) And I turn back round and just listen – won't let no dickhead take this away from me. Candy sings one more line, the song ends, and that's that.

Fucking Chris.

But then, summat weird happens...

Candy gets right off stage and wraps her arms around me.

Every part of me freezes up – except me heart which is beating like it's trying to burst out of me body just to be closer to her.

'Hi, I'm Candy,' she says.

I try not to lose me head.

(*frozen uncomfortably, to CANDY*) Billy, what are you doing?

So Chris is like: 'Mate, this is what I were trying to say. I bet Billy twenty quid he couldn't be Candy the whole night. Easiest smackers I ever made, lad. Weeeey.'

*WILL gives the audience an 'I know, right?' look. Then:*

So, Candy's all, 'I'm sorry, I don't know a Billy. I'm Candy.'

It's a fucking nightmare! What am I going to do now?

I remember why I'm here in the first place – Dutch courage: I say, 'Hi, I'm Will'.

*He sticks his hand out for a handshake.*

She shakes me hand.

Then we chat for about half an hour!

*WILL is elated. Perhaps he rubs his handshook hand's fingers together sensuously.*

I ask her about herself – where she grew up, what kind of music she's into... All that stuff Romeo should've asked Juliet.

At the back of me head I know it's Billy making it up on the spot, but in my state I think if this is how he sees that little part of himself that I love then it *is* real. Everything she's saying.

Then, she does that thing what lasses do when they want to sleep with ya – ever-so-slightly brushes my hand with her fingers. Shivers all down me spine!

Anyway, I need a piss by this point so I head to the gents.

*He acts this out. Maybe even finds an audience member to use as a urinal.*

There's a mirror above the urinal, right, so as I piss I look at myself and I say, (*pointing at himself in the mirror*) I say 'you *have* to tell her.'

So I go back and I grab Candy by the arm – I'd washed me hands, obviously – and I...

*WILL stops in his tracks, looking up at the back of the audience.*

*He breathes in and out, calming down. He doesn't want to say this next part, but he knows he has to.*

I grab her arm and I say...

*He breathes in. Out. In. Then he spills his guts out:*

I say, 'Candy, listen, I know you're Billy, really. But I also know that there is part of you that is Candy, that is real. And I love that part of you. I love you, Candy. I know I sound like I'm fucking crazy right now, but I don't care. I wanna be with ya. If that meant never seeing Billy again, so be it. All I know is that I feel something, and I think you feel it too. Just tell me it in't all an act. Because this is real to me. The realest thing I've ever known. Please.'

*A long pause.*

*Then...*

(*as BILLY*) 'What the fuck, Will? Are you having a laugh?'

All of a sudden: Billy... in a dress. He starts backing away, takes his wig off.

*Pause. WILL shrugs.*

Chris gets his twenty quid.

*WILL nods to himself, taking in the rejection.*

I fuck off. Obviously.

When I get back, me Mum's still up. Think she's almost as fucked as me.

I ask her what she were gonna say to me before. About Toadface.

She says: 'Will, your uncle Teddy made her happy. But it meant she never learnt – it's summat you have to work at – being happy alone.'

(*his voice breaking*) And I just can't hear that. Not now. I hug her with all me might and I cry in her arms.

I say 'I don't wanna be alone. And I ain't been happy since I were a boy. I thought I had a chance tonight. I thought I did. I thought... I...'

*WILL sits down, perhaps wiping teary eyes.*

*He stays seated for a while, collecting his thoughts.*

A couple days later, Billy texts me. Says he's sorry. His reaction. He were just shocked – it were intense, he says. He wants to meet up, talk about it.

I don't reply and a week later he sends another one: "Pint Tuesday? We can talk about it or not, whatever you want."

I ignore it. Then the lads are going for pints, ask if I'm coming. I ignore them, archive the group chat.

After a month I know the silence is getting suspicious so I start replying saying I'm "too tired, work's been mad."

Debra's hesitant to let me back in, but I know she needs the extra manpower. I'm not what I was before all this, but I'm getting into the swing of it.

Billy tries to call me a couple of times. I let it ring out. One day I wake up to a text from him, sent at three in the morning on a Friday night. It says:

"Hey Will, I hope you know you can love whatever kind of person you want. The thing is with Candy though is it's always me behind the wheel. For me that's as far as it goes. I'm sorry, mate. Thinking of you – hope you're looking after yourself. Please don't be a stranger."

I think about replying sometimes.

*He shakes his head.*

Eventually, I stop having those dreams. But then last night, I have a new one.

I'm sitting on Toadface's chair, watching telly. And I don't know when it starts but Candy's singing. It's a live TV performance.

I can't touch her. I can't be close to her. I can only watch her, listen to her.

And I think: what if this is as close as I'll ever get? No ten years of marriage, not even what me Mum and Dad had. Just this.

I'm thinking this and I'm sitting there, once again crying to the sound of Candy's voice. And I realise no one really knows anyone, do they. We can only ever go off of what's right there in front of us.

And maybe the girl I love's not real, maybe I made her up – but she gave me something I needed, something that was missing – made me feel... *alive* again.

And at least I told her, y'know, that I loved her. That has to count for something.

And now I'm sinking into Toadface's chair, deeper and deeper, and know I can let it happen or I can pull myself up to my feet and walk away. I hear Candy's voice calling me down towards her and this feeling comes over me; this feeling of pure bliss, like.. I don't know...

Then I wake up.

*CUT TO BLACK.*

# END

# ALSO AVAILABLE FROM SALAMANDER STREET

*All Salamander Street plays can be bought in bulk at a discount for performance or study. Contact info@salamanderstreet com to enquire about performance liscenses.*

### Cowboys and Lesbians by Billie Esplen
ISBN: 9781914228902

Queer romantic comedy which examines the intersection between sexuality and fantasy through the eyes of two closeted teenage girls writing a parody American coming-of-age romance.

### Ode to Joy (How Gordon got to go to the nasty pig party) by James Ley
ISBN: 9781914228681

LGBTQ play about love, friendship and Schokoladenkuchen, described by The Scotsman as 'a filthy and brilliantly-paced joyride.'

### If You Love Me This Might Hurt by Matty May
ISBN: 9781914228513

An uncensored and funny solo show about rage, suicide and so-called self-care. Matty dismantles the roots of the problem that could actually enable everyone to put their mental health first.

### Chatsky and Miser, Miser! by Anthony Burgess
ISBN: 9781914228889

Anthony Burgess expertly tackles the major monuments of French and Russian theatre: *The Miser* by Molière and *Chatsky* by Alexander Griboyedov. Burgess's recently discovered verse and prose plays are published for the first time in this volume.

### Class by Scottee
ISBN: 9781913630010

Solo show about what it is to be embarrassed about where you're from, how you can pretend to be richer than you are and explores why we all get a thrill from watching how he other half live.